Published in 2012 by Helen Exley Giftbooks.

Design selection and arrangement copyright © Helen Exley Creative Ltd 2012.

Copyright © Helen Exley Creative Ltd 2012.

Photographs by Richard Exley © Helen Exley Creative Ltd 2012.

12 11 10 9 8 7 6 5 4 3 2 1

ISBN 978-1-84634-551-7

**Helen Exley Giftbooks,
16 Chalk Hill, Watford, Herts WD19 4BG, UK.
www.helenexleygiftbooks.com**

A gift of
CALM

A HELEN EXLEY GIFTBOOK

INTRODUCTION

You have a tiny book in your
hands. But in these 240 pages
you have a wonderful collection
of the very best, most thoughtful
words ever written about calm,
about peace and quiet beauty,
about meditation and wisdom.
This is a book to dip into again
and again, just to celebrate the
wonder of existence...
then take the sense of peace
within these pages out into
the hectic world around you.

Thoughts on
DEEP PEACE...

Calm is a clear
well that you may
draw from whenever
you have need.

MAYA V. PATEL, B.1943

*M*ay peace
and peace
and peace
be everywhere.

THE UPANISHADS
(C.900-600 BC)

Let your mind be quiet,
realizing the beauty
of the world, and
the immense, the boundless
treasures that it holds in
store. All that you have
within you,
all that your heart desires,

all that your nature so
specially fits you for
– that waits embedded
in the great whole,
for you. It will surely
come to you. It will
surely come to you.

EDWARD CARPENTER

ALL PROBLEMS
FADE OUT IN
PROPORTION AS YOU
DEVELOP THIS ABILITY
TO BE QUIET,
TO BEHOLD
AND TO WITNESS
DIVINE HARMONY
UNFOLD.

JOEL S. GOLDSMITH

You ask why I make
my home in the mountain
forest, and I smile,
and am silent, and even
my soul remains quiet:
it lives in the other world
which no one owns.
The peach trees blossom.
The water flows.

LI PO

Peace is when time doesn't matter as it passes by.

MARIA SCHELL,
QUOTED IN "TIME",
MARCH 3, 1958

Deep in the soul, below pain,
below all the
distraction of life,
is a silence vast and grand
— an infinite ocean

of calm, which nothing
can disturb. Nature's
own exceeding peace,
which "passes
understanding".

C.M.C. QUOTED IN R.M. BUCKE

Only in
Quietness can
the Infinity
of Wonder
Find You.

PAM BROWN, B.1928

*L*isten in deep silence.
Be very still and open your
mind... Sink deep into the
peace that waits for you
beyond the frantic, riotous
thoughts and sights and
sounds of this insane world.

FROM
"A COURSE IN MIRACLES"

*That which we seek
with passionate
longing, here
and there, upward
and outward;
we find at last
within ourselves.*

C.M.C.
QUOTED IN R.M. BUCKE

There is a silence into which the world cannot intrude. There is an ancient peace you carry in your heart and have not lost.

FROM
"A COURSE IN MIRACLES"

*B*efore me peaceful
Behind me peaceful
Under me peaceful
Over me peaceful
Around me peaceful.

NAVAJO PRAYER

LIKE WATER WHICH
CAN CLEARLY
MIRROR THE SKY
AND THE TREES ONLY
SO LONG AS ITS SURFACE
IS UNDISTURBED,

THE MIND CAN
ONLY REFLECT
THE TRUE IMAGE OF
THE SELF WHEN
IT IS TRANQUIL AND
WHOLLY RELAXED.

INDRA DEVI (1899-2002)

LIE GENTLY IN THE
DARK AND LISTEN TO
THE RAIN, THE SWISH
OF PASSING CARS,
THE HUSH OF LEAVES.
RENOUNCE DECISIONS,
SPECULATION,
THE TUG OF TIME.
THE WORLD BEYOND
THE WINDOW ENFOLDS
YOUR SILENCE,
HOLDS YOU SOFTLY.

PAM BROWN, B.1928

*The heart
of the wise
person
lies quiet like
limpid water.*

CAMEROONIAN
SAYING

The clear river curves
around our village:
these long summer
days are beautiful, indeed.

Swallows swoop from
the eaves, the gulls all
flock to the water.

This medicine is all a sick
man needs. What man
could ask for more?

TU FU

HERE, NOW, TODAY...

NOTHING
IS WORTH MORE
THAN THIS DAY.

JOHANN WOLFGANG VON GOETHE
(1749-1832)

*That it will never
come again
is what makes
life so sweet.*

EMILY DICKINSON
(1830-1886)

To see a World in a Grain of Sand And a Heaven in a Wild Flower, Hold infinity in the palm of your hand and Eternity in an hour.

WILLIAM BLAKE (1757-1827)

The lure of the
distant and the difficult
is deceptive.
The great opportunity
is where you are.

JOHN BURROUGHS (1837-1921)

*We need time
to dream,
time to remember,
and time
to reach the infinite.
Time to be.*

GLADYS TABER
(1899-1980)

If you want to be happy, be.

LEO TOLSTOY
(1828-1910)

You can destroy your now by worrying about tomorrow.

JANIS JOPLIN
(1943-1970)

Yesterday
is a cancelled
cheque; tomorrow
is a promissory note;
today is
the only cash
you have – so spend
it wisely.

KAY LYONS

*Living the past
is a dull and lonely
business,
looking back strains
the neck muscles,
causes you to
bump into people
not going your way.*

EDNA FERBER
(1885-1968)

We loiter
IN WINTER WHILE IT
IS ALREADY SPRING.

HENRY DAVID THOREAU
(1817-1862)

*T*he way to use life
is to do nothing
through acting, The way
to use life is to do
everything through being.

LAO-TZU
(6TH CENTURY B.C.)

Sitting silently,
Doing nothing,
Spring comes,
And the grass
grows by itself.

BASHO (1644-1694)

GENTLENESS...

Nothing
IS SO STRONG
AS GENTLENESS;
NOTHING SO
GENTLE AS REAL
STRENGTH.

ST FRANCIS DE SALES
(1567-1622)

The one
who smiles
rather than rages
is always
the stronger.

JAPANESE WISDOM

In this world there is nothing softer or thinner than water. But to compel the hard and unyielding, it has no equal. That the weak overcomes the strong, that the hard gives way to the gentle — This everyone knows, yet no one acts accordingly.

LAO-TZU
(6TH CENTURY B.C.)

There is in all things
an inexhaustible
sweetness and purity,
a silence that is
a fountain of action
and joy.

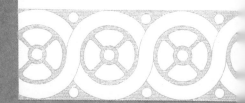

It rises up in wordless
gentleness
and flows out to me
from unseen roots
of all created being.

THOMAS MERTON (1915-1968)

In a gentle
WAY YOU
CAN SHAKE
THE WORLD.

MAHATMA GANDHI
(1869-1948)

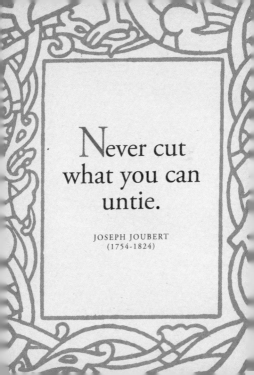

Never cut
what you can
untie.

JOSEPH JOUBERT
(1754-1824)

Dripping water
hollows out
a stone,
a ring is worn
away by use.

OVID (43 B.C.–17 A.D.)

*Strong in
their softness are
the sprays of
the wisteria creeper;
The pine in
its hardness is broken
by the weak snow.*

MASTER JUKYU

Nature chose for a tool,
not the earthquake
or lightning to rend
and split asunder, not
the stormy torrent
or eroding rain,
but the tender snow
flowers noiselessly
falling through
unnumbered centuries.

JOHN MUIR (1838-1914)

*Loud words fall
resoundingly into
nothingness.
The right word even
spoken quietly, will
enlighten the world.*

MAHABHARATAM

*Better than
a thousand useless
words is
one single word
that gives peace.*

THE DHAMMAPADA

Take the
GENTLE PATH.

GEORGE HERBERT
(1593-1633)

NATURE'S PEACE...

*Once you have heard
the meadowlark
and caught the scent
of fresh-plowed earth,
peace cannot escape you.*

SEQUICHIE

Over all the mountaintops
Is peace.
In all treetops
You perceive Scarcely
a breath.
The little birds
in the forest are silent.
Wait then; soon you, too,
will have peace.

JOHANN WOLFGANG
VON GOETHE (1749-1832)

*W*hatever peace
I know rests in
the natural world,
in feeling myself
a part of it, even
in a small way.

MAY SARTON
(1912-1995)

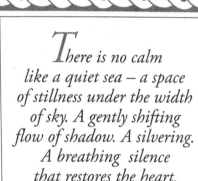

*T*here is no calm
like a quiet sea – a space
of stillness under the width
of sky. A gently shifting
flow of shadow. A silvering.
A breathing silence
that restores the heart.

PAM BROWN, B.1928

THE MORNING
SUN, THE NEW
SWEET EARTH
AND THE
GREAT SILENCE.

T.C. MCLUHAN

A person is blessed
who every day is
permitted to behold
anything so pure and
serene
as the western sky
at sunset, while
revolutions
vex the world.

HENRY DAVID THOREAU (1817-1862)

I lay in a meadow until
the unwrinkled serenity
entered into my bones,
and made me into one
with the browsing kine,
the still greenery,
the drifting clouds,
and the swooping birds.

ALICE JAMES (1848-1892)

SILENCE...

Much
silence has
a mighty
noise.

SWAHILI PROVERB

Silence
is more musical
than any song.

CHRISTINA ROSSETTI
(1830-1894)

THE QUIETER
YOU BECOME
THE MORE
YOU CAN HEAR.

BABA RAM DASS

Learn to be silent.
Let your mind listen
and absorb.

PYTHAGORAS

*Every moment
there is news coming
out of silence.*

RAINER MARIA RILKE
(1875-1926)

Our greatest experiences are our quietest moments.

FRIEDERICH NIETZSCHE
(1844-1900)

One of the greatest sounds of them all — and to me it is a sound — is utter, complete silence.

ANDRE KOSTELANETZ

*The words
the happy say
are paltry melody.
But those
the silent feel
are beautiful.*

EMILY DICKINSON
(1830-1886)

We eat in silence,
quietly smoke a pipe,
and depart.
Thus is our host honored.
This is not the way of
the white man.
After his food has been
eaten, one is expected
to say foolish things.
Then the host feels honored.

FOUR GUNS
NATIVE AMERICAN

Listen!
Or your tongue
will make
you deaf.

CHEROKEE SAYING

Silence is deep as Eternity; speech, shallow as Time.

THOMAS CARLYLE
(1795-1881)

Grant yourself a moment of peace and you will understand how foolishly you have scurried about. Learn to be silent and you will notice that you have talked too much.

TSCHEN TSCHI JU

W E FILL UP EMPTINESS
WITH NOISE, WHICH LEAVES
NO ROOM
FOR SOMETHING NEW
AND WONDERFUL TO GROW.

PAM BROWN, B.1928

*...there is a luxury
in being quiet
in the heart of chaos.*

VIRGINIA WOOLF
(1882-1941)

AND SILENCE
LIKE A POULTICE, COMES
TO HEAL THE BLOWS
OF SOUND.

OLIVER WENDELL HOLMES
(1809-1894)

*We do not remember
in old age the shouting of
the pleasure beach – but
the stumbling of a bumble bee
along a window pane and
summer sun and quietness.*

PAM BROWN, B.1928

SACRED IDLENESS!

Work is not always required of us. There is such thing as sacred idleness, the cultivation of which is now fearfully neglected.

GEORGE MACDONALD
(1824–1905)

I loafe and invite my soul...

WALT WHITMAN
(1819-1892)

If you can spend a perfectly useless afternoon in a perfectly useless manner, you have learned how to live.

LIN YUTANG (1895-1976)

I leave this notice
on my door...
"I am gone
into the fields
To take what this
sweet hour yields,
Reflection,

you may come
tomorrow,
Expectation, too,
be off!
Today is for
itself enough."

PERCY BYSSHE
SHELLEY (1792-1822)

LIFE IS EATING US UP.
WE SHALL BE FABLES
PRESENTLY. KEEP COOL:
IT WILL BE ALL
ONE A HUNDRED
YEARS HENCE.

RALPH WALDO EMERSON
(1803-1882)

*Life is so short
we must move very slowly.*

THAI PROVERB

IF YOU ARE LOSING
YOUR LEISURE,
LOOK OUT!
YOU ARE LOSING
YOUR SOUL.

LOGAN PEARSALL SMITH
(1865-1946)

Life isn't
a matter
of milestones
but of
moments.

ROSE FITZGERALD
KENNEDY

I EXPAND
AND LIVE IN
THE WARM DAY
LIKE CORN
AND MELONS.

RALPH WALDO EMERSON
(1803-1882)

Take time to be
friendly – it is the road
to happiness. Take time
to dream – it is hitching
your wagon to a star.
Take time to love
and to be loved – it is

the privilege of the gods.
Take time to look
around – it is too short
a day to be selfish.
Take time to laugh –
it is the music of
the soul.

OLD ENGLISH

Life just is.
You have to flow with it.
Give yourself
to the moment.
Let it happen.

GOVENOR
JERRY BROWN, B.1938

There is great happiness
in not wanting,
in not being something,
in not going somewhere.

J. KRISHNAMURTI
(1895-1986)

L<small>ET MY DOING</small>
<small>NOTHING WHEN</small>
I <small>HAVE NOTHING</small>
<small>TO DO BECOME</small>
<small>UNTROUBLED</small>
<small>IN ITS DEPTH OF</small>

PEACE LIKE
THE EVENING IN
THE SEASHORE
WHEN THE WATER
IS SILENT.

RABINDRANATH TAGORE
(1861-1941)

BEING LOST IN BEAUTY...

The hours
when the mind
is absorbed
by beauty
are the only
hours we live.

RICHARD JEFFERIES
(1848-1887)

What life can compare
to this? Sitting quietly
by the window,
I watch the leaves fall
and the flowers bloom,
As the seasons
come and go.

HSUEH-TOU (982-1052)

*T*raining began with children who were taught to sit still and enjoy it. They were taught to use their organs of smell, to look where there was apparently nothing to see, and to listen intently when all seemingly was quiet.

LUTHER STANDING BEAR (1868-1939),
OGLALA SIOUX CHIEF

It is good to be alone
in a garden at dawn
or dark so that all its
shy presences may haunt
you and possess you
in a reverie of suspended
thought.

JAMES DOUGLAS

Quieten your mind
and close your eyes.
Be still.
Feel the sun upon
your face.
Hear the shrill
of bird song.
Rejoice in your senses.
Rejoice in life.

PAM BROWN, B.1928

*You do not need to leave
your room...
Remain sitting
at your table and listen.
Do not even listen,
simply wait.
Do not even wait,
be quite still and solitary.
The world will freely offer
itself to you. It will roll
in ecstasy at your feet.*

FRANZ KAFKA (1883-1924)

I have learned to have
very modest goals for society
and myself;
things like clean air,
green grass, children with
bright eyes, not being pushed
around, useful work that
suits one's abilities
and plain tasty food...

PAUL GOODMAN (1911-1972)

We collect data, things, people, ideas, "profound experiences", never penetrating any of them... But there are times when we stop. We sit still.

We lose ourselves in a
pile of leaves or its
memory. We listen
and breezes from a
whole other world begin
to whisper.

JAMES CARROLL, B.1943

BEING
ALONE...

What a lovely surprise
to discover
how un-lonely being alone
can be.

ELLEN BURSTYN, B.1932

*T*rue peace of mind
and complete tranquillity
are only to be found
in solitude.

ARTHUR SCHOPENHAUER
(1788-1860)

Our language has wisely sensed the two sides of being alone. It has created the word "loneliness" to express the pain of being alone. And it has created the word "solitude" to express the glory of being alone.

PAUL TILLICH (1886-1965)

In solitude,
where we are
LEAST
alone.

*T*he cure for all
the illness of life
is stored in the inner
depth of life itself,
the access to which
becomes possible
when we are alone.
This solitude is

*a world in itself,
full of wonders
and resources unthought
of. It is absurdly near;
yet so
unapproachably
distant.*

RABINDRANATH TAGORE
(1861-1941)

Solitude, quality solitude, is an assertion of self-worth, because only in the stillness can we hear the truth of our own unique voices.

PEARL CLEAGE

Solitude gives birth to the original in us, to beauty unfamiliar and perilous.

THOMAS MANN
(1875-1955)

*W*e cannot long
survive without air,
water, and sleep.
Next in importance comes
food. And close on its
heels, solitude.

THOMAS SZASZ

When I am,
completely myself,
entirely alone,
and of good cheer...
it is on such occasions
that ideas flow best
and most abundantly.

WOLFGANG AMADEUS
MOZART (1756-1791)

I suppose –
the moments one most
enjoys are moments –
alone – when one
unexpectedly stretches
something inside
you that needs
stretching.

GEORGIA O'KEEFFE
(1887-1986)

*H*ave the courage
to be alone... for once
try to endure your own
company for a while....
Don't speak, then,
not even with yourself
nor with the others
with whom we dispute
even when they are
not there. Wait. Listen....
Endure yourself!

K. RAHNER
(1904-1984)

It is in deep solitude
that I find the gentleness
with which I can truly love
my brothers. The more solitary
I am, the more affection
I have for them. It is pure
affection and filled with
reverence for the solitudes
of others.

THOMAS MERTON
(1915-1968)

The best thinking
has been done in solitude.
The worst
has been done in turmoil.

THOMAS EDISON (1847-1931)

Everlasting truth can only
be heard in solitude.

MEISTER ECKART (C.1260-1328)

It is easy
in the world to live
after the world's
opinion; it is easy
in solitude to live
after our own;
but the great person

is one who
in the midst of
the crowd keeps
with perfect sweetness
the independence
of solitude.

RALPH WALDO
EMERSON (1803-1882)

THE SIMPLE WAY

Poor and content
is rich, and
rich enough.

WILLIAM SHAKESPEARE
(1564-1616)

*To be without
some of the things
you want is an
indispensable part
of happiness.*

BERTRAND RUSSELL
(1872-1970)

A DIAMOND
LIES ABOUT THE NECK
AS AN ANXIETY
A DAISY CHAIN
AS A BLESSING.

PAM BROWN, B.1928

*L*et your boat
of life be light,
packed only with
what you need —
a homely home
and simple pleasures,
one or two friends
worth the name,

*someone to love
and to love you,
a cat, a dog,
enough to eat
and enough to wear.*

JEROME K. JEROME
(1859-1927)

He or she who knows
that enough is enough
will always have enough.

LAO-TZU
(6TH CENTURY B.C.)

You can't have everything.
Where would you put it?

ANN LANDERS
(1918-2002)

He knew how
to be poor without
the least hint of squalor
or inelegance....
He chose to be rich
by making his wants few.

RALPH WALDO EMERSON
(1803-1882),
ABOUT HENRY DAVID THOREAU

*N*othing will
content him
who is not
content with
a little.

GREEK PROVERB

HE THAT PILES UP TREASURE HAS MUCH TO LOSE.

LAO-TZU
(6TH CENTURY B.C.)

We spend our
lives accumulating
things, as
a bower bird,
– but there comes
a time when
they become too
heavy a burden

– and we must
give them back
to the world.
Gaining freedom.

PAM BROWN, B.1928

LESS
IS
MORE.

ROBERT BROWNING
(1812-1889)

The greatest wealth is contentment with a little.

PROVERB

BEING STILL...

THE GREATEST REVELATION IS STILLNESS.

LAO-TZU
(6TH CENTURY B.C.)

*To a mind
that is still
the whole universe
surrenders.*

CHUANG TZU

*The miracle
comes quietly into
the mind that stops
an instant
and is still.*

FROM
"A COURSE IN MIRACLES"

THE TRAIL
IS BEAUTIFUL.
BE STILL.

ANONYMOUS, DAKOTA

Without stirring abroad
one can know
the whole world;
Without looking out of
the window one can see
the way of heaven.
The further one goes
the less one knows.

LAO-TZU
(6TH CENTURY B.C.)

All our miseries
derive from
not being able
to sit quiet
in a room alone.

BLAISE PASCAL
(1623-1662)

*H*ow can the world
know peace when we have
lost the gift of stillness?

MAYA V. PATEL, B.1943

*M*y greatest wealth
is the great stillness
in which I strive and
grow and win what the world
cannot take from me
with fire or sword.

JOHANN WOLFGANG VON GOETHE
(1749-1832)

Not all of us can find an outer place of peace – but be still. Here are the desert silences, the murmuring oceans, the wind-brushed moors, the mountain tops, all held in the centre of your being.

PAM BROWN, B.1928

Stay quiet;
refuse nothing; flowers
grow only because they
tranquilly allow the
sun's rays to reach them.
You must do the same.

JULIANA KRUDENER
(1764-1824)

*Teach me the art of creating
islands of stillness, in which
I can absorb the beauty of
everyday things: clouds, trees,
a snatch of music...*

MARION STROUD

Here will we sit
and let the sounds of music
Creep in our ears: soft
stillness and the night
Become the touches of
sweet harmony.

WILLIAM SHAKESPEARE (1564-1616),
FROM "THE MERCHANT OF VENICE"

COMING AWAY FROM THE DIN

Once you plant deep the longing for peace, confusion leaves of itself.

SENG TS'AN

*C*ome away from the din.
Come away to the quiet
fields, over which the great
sky stretches, and where,
between us, and the stars,
there lies but silence;
and there, in the stillness
let us listen to the voice that
is speaking within us.

JEROME K. JEROME
(1859-1927)

Serenity does not cancel
hope or adventure,
work or love. It flows
through the landscape
of our busy lives,
quiet and strong.
Clear and gentle. Refreshing
all we do or dream.

PAM BROWN, B. 1928

...To preserve
the silence within
– amid all the noise.
To remain open
and quiet,...
no matter how

many tramp across
the parade-ground
in whirling dust
under an arid sky.

DAG HAMMARSKJÖLD
(1905-1961)

The serene
have not opted out of life.
They see more widely,
love more dearly,
rejoice in the things
the frantic mind
no longer sees or hears.

PAM BROWN, B.1928

Though we travel
the world over to find
the beautiful,
we must carry it with us
or we find it not.

RALPH WALDO EMERSON
(1803-1882)

*There is a quietness,
a contentment,
at the heart
of all that is —
beneath the noise
and bustle,
the excitements
and the terrors.*

CHARLOTTE GRAY

Why should we be in such desperate haste to succeed, and in such desperate enterprises? If a man cannot keep pace with his companions, perhaps it is because he hears a different drummer. Let him step to the music which he hears...

HENRY DAVID THOREAU
(1817-1862)

Even in the heart of a city
there can be a place of calm.
Doors shut and curtains
closed, a light against
the dark, wrapped round in
dear, accustomed things,
we can withdraw
and find ourselves again.

PAM BROWN, B.1928

Do NOT LET TRIFLES
DISTURB YOUR TRANQUILLITY
OF MIND... LIFE IS
TOO PRECIOUS TO BE
SACRIFICED
FOR THE NONESSENTIAL
AND TRANSIENT...

GRENVILLE KLEISER

If there is tumult in your heart seek out tranquillity, – a calm and moonlit sea, a place of peace, a gentleness of landscape – and let their quietness flow through you, and wash your care away.

PAM BROWN, B.1928

*Don't hurry,
don't worry.
You're only here
for a short visit.
So be sure to stop
and smell
the flowers.*

WALTER HAGEN
(1892-1969)

BEING HAPPY WHERE YOU ARE...

And so, while others miserably pledge themselves to the insatiable pursuit of ambition and brief power, I will be stretched out in the shade, singing.

FRAY LUIS DE LEÓN (C. 1527-1591)

Drinking tea,
eating rice,
I pass my time
as it comes;
Looking down
at the stream,
Looking up
at the mountain,
How serene and
relaxed I feel indeed!

PAO-TZU WEN-CH'I (C.900)

*Simplify. Stop bothering
with the non-essentials.
Having devoted my life
to my work so far,
I should reap the harvest
and learn how to live the rest
of it properly. It's time now
for trees and grass
and growing things.*

AUTHOR UNKNOWN

The best things are nearest:
breath in your nostrils, light
in your eyes, flowers at your
feet, duties at your hand...
Do not grasp at the stars,
but do life's plain common work
as it comes, certain that daily
duties and daily bread
are the sweetest things in life.

ROBERT LOUIS
STEVENSON (1850-1894)

Do nondoing,
strive for nonstriving,
savour the flavourless, regard
the small as important,
make much of little,
repay enmity with virtue;
plan for difficulty when
it is still easy, do the great
while it is still small.

LAO-TZU
(6TH CENTURY B.C.)

Change is
an easy panacea.
It takes character
to stay in one place
and be
happy there.

ELIZABETH
CLARKE DUNN

I do not want change.
I want the same old and loved
things, the same trees and soft
ashgreen; the turtle-doves,
the yellow-hammer singing
so long as there is light to cast
a shadow, for such is
the measure of his song, and
I want them in the same place.

RICHARD JEFFERIES (1848-1887)

*I*t becomes necessary to
learn how to clear the mind
of all clouds, to free it
of all useless ballast
and debris by dismissing
the burden of too much
concern with material things.

INDRA DEVI (1899-2002)

I believe we would
be happier to have
a personal revolution
in our lives and go
back to simpler living.
It is the simple things
of life that make

living worthwhile,
the sweet fundamental
things such as love
and duty, work and
rest and living close
to nature.

LAURA INGALLS WILDER
(1867-1957)

...how many of us live our life as if it is a product? When we get or have what we want: a better job, a new place to live, thinner, smarter,

older (younger?),
serenity, peace, etc.
etc., then we'll really
have something.
Only then our lives
will be worth living.

JAN JOHNSON DRANTELL

No land belongs
unto me, Yet I can go
out in the meadows
and see the healthy green
grass – and behold the
shower fall,
And he that feels this,
who can say he is poor?

JOHN CLARE
(1793-1864)

Do not seek to have everything that happens happen as you wish, but wish for everything to happen as it actually does happen, and your life will be serene.

EPICTETUS (C.55-135A.D.)

I laugh when I hear that
the fish in the water is thirsty.
You don't grasp the fact
that what is most alive
of all is inside your own house;
and so you walk from one
holy city to the next with
a confused – look!

KABIR (1440-1518)

*The tipi is much better
to live in; always clean,
warm in winter,
cool in summer; easy to
move. The [modern]
man builds big house,
cost much money, like big
cage, shut out sun,
can never move;
always sick.*

CHIEF FLYING HAWK
(1852-1931)

I USED TO BELIEVE
THAT ANYTHING WAS BETTER
THAN NOTHING. NOW
I KNOW THAT SOMETIMES
NOTHING IS BETTER.

GLENDA JACKSON, B.1936

Life's sweetest
things are
the quietest
things...
A happy life
consists
of tranquillity
of mind.

CICERO (106-143 B.C.)

[Happiness] is the flower of a long inner life of joy and contentment; it tells of peaceful hours and days on the sunniest heights of our soul.

COUNT
MAURICE MAETERLINCK
(1862-1949)

To have peace
in one's
soul is the greatest
happiness.

ORIENTAL WISDOM

True joy is serene.

SENECA (c.55 B.C. – c.40A.D.)

Happiness is
as a butterfly,
which, when pursued,
is always
beyond our grasp,

but which, if you
will sit down
quietly, may
alight upon you.

NATHANIEL HAWTHORNE
(1804-1864)

He is happiest,
be he king
or peasant,
who finds peace
in his home.

JOHANN
WOLFGANG VON GOETHE
(1749-1832)

To watch the corn grow,
and the blossoms set;
to draw hard breath over
ploughshare or spade;
to read, to think, to love,
to hope, to pray, –
these are the things
that make us happy.

JOHN RUSKIN (1819-1900)

I hope you find
joy in the great
things of life
– but also in
the little things.
A flower,
a song, a butterfly
on your hand.

ELLEN LEVINE

True happiness is of
a retired nature, and an
enemy to pomp and noise;
it arises, in the first place,
from the enjoyment
of one's self; and in the next,
from the friendship
and conversation
of a select few companions.

JOSEPH ADDISON
(1672-1719)

The struggle, the courage,
the exploration
that make up our lives
have no purpose
if they do not lead
to quietness of mind and
the joy of tranquillity.

PAM BROWN, B.1928

What a fine lesson
is conveyed to the mind –
to watch only for the smiles
and neglect the frowns of fate,
to compose our lives
of bright and gentle moments,
turning always to the
sunny side of things,
and letting the rest slip from
our imaginations, unheeded
or forgotten.

WILLIAM HAZLITT (1778-1830)

Peace is the fairest form of happiness.

WILLIAM ELLERY
CHANNING (1780-1842)

LET IT BE...

*D*o what you can,
with what you have,
where you are.

THEODORE ROOSEVELT
(1858-1919)

The miracle
is not to fly
in the air,
or to walk
on the water,
but to walk
on the earth.

CHINESE PROVERB

I had been my
repeated experience
that when you said
to life calmly and firmly
(but very firmly!),
"I trust you;
do what you must,"
life had an uncanny way
of responding to
your need.

OLGA ILYIN

*Joy exists
only in
self acceptance.
Seek perfect
acceptance,
not a perfect life.*

AUTHOR UNKNOWN

To EVERYTHING THERE IS A SEASON, AND A TIME TO EVERY PURPOSE UNDER HEAVEN.

ECCLESIASTES
3, 1-8.

*C*ontentment comes
as the infallible result
of great acceptances,
great humilities —
of not trying to make
ourselves this or that
(to conform to some

dramatized version of ourselves), but of surrendering ourselves to the fullness of life — of letting life flow through us.

DAVID GRAYSON (1870-1946)

To be content
with what we possess
is the greatest
and most secure
of riches.

MARCUS TULLIUS
CICERO
(106-43 B.C.)

I know not how it is
with you – I love the first
and last, the whole field
of the present view,
the whole flow of the past.
Nor should you change,
nor I, one pebble in our
path – one star. In all our
heaven of sky.

ROBERT
LOUIS STEVENSON
(1850-1894)

*G*od grant me serenity
to accept the things I cannot
change, courage to change
the things I can, and wisdom
to know the difference.

WILLIAM JAMES (1842-1910)

*C*ontentment is
the philosopher's stone,
which turn all it toucheth
into gold; the poor man
is rich with it, the rich man
poor without it.

PROVERB

Those who face
that which is actually
before them,
unburdened by the
past, undistracted
by the future,

these are they
who live...
these are those who
have found the
secret of contentment.

ALBAN GOODIER,
FROM "THE SCHOOL OF LOVE"

WHAT IS A HELEN EXLEY GIFTBOOK?

Helen Exley Giftbooks cover
the most powerful of all human
relationships: the bonds within
families and between friends,
and the themes of personal values,
peace and wisdom.
No expense is spared in making sure
that each book is as meaningful
a gift as it is possible to create:
good to give, good to receive.
If you have loved it – tell others!
There is no power on earth
like the word-of-mouth
recommendation of friends!

Acknowledgements:

The publishers are grateful for permission to reproduce
copyright material. Whilst every reasonable effort has been
made to trace copyright holders, the publishers would
be pleased to hear from any not here acknowledged.

All text by Pam Brown, Charlotte Gray, and
Maya V. Patel: © Helen Exley Creative Ltd. 2012.

Photographs by Richard Exley
© Helen Exley Creative Ltd. 2012.

Images from the Dover Pictorial Archive Series.

Helen Exley Giftbooks
16 Chalk Hill,
Watford, Herts
WD19 4BG, UK

www.helenexleygiftbooks.com